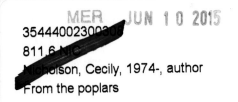

MER   JUN 10 2015

35444002300~~~~~~

811.6 NIC~~~~

Nicholson, Cecily, 1974-, author

From the poplars

FROM THE POPLARS

D0793069

Cecily Nicholson's
Triage is also available
from Talonbooks

FROM THE
POPLARS

CECILY
NICHOLSON

Talonbooks

Thompson-Nicola Regional District
Library System
300 - 465 VICTORIA STREET
KAMLOOPS, B.C. V2C 2A9

© 2014 Cecily Nicholson

All rights reserved. No part of this book may be reproduced, stored in a retrieval system, or transmitted, in any form or by any means, without the prior written consent of the publisher or a licence from Access Copyright (The Canadian Copyright Licensing Agency). For a copyright licence, visit accesscopyright.ca or call toll free to 1-800-893-5777.

Talonbooks
278 East First Avenue, Vancouver, British Columbia, Canada V5T 1A6
www.talonbooks.com

First printing: 2014

Typeset in Adobe Caslon
Printed and bound in Canada on 100% post-consumer recycled paper

Cover design by Typesmith
Cover photograph by Andy Simonds

Talonbooks gratefully acknowledges the financial support of the Canada Council for the Arts, the Government of Canada through the Canada Book Fund, and the Province of British Columbia through the British Columbia Arts Council and the Book Publishing Tax Credit.

Library and Archives Canada Cataloguing in Publication

Nicholson, Cecily, 1974–, author
       From the poplars / Cecily Nicholson.

Poems.
ISBN 978-0-88922-856-6 (pbk.)

       1. Poplar Island (B.C. : Island)—Poetry.
I. Title.

PS8627.I2393F76 2014   C811'.6   C2014-901355-8

3 5444 00230030 8

"The island," I am told, "is not for sale." I am surprised to be mistaken for a potential buyer. At Planning, their recollections of the place are of ownership and "issues." I describe my project and they express a kind curiosity, perhaps even delight. How to say, then, that this effort is an outcrop of disunity—a gross sense of settlement in the Royal City, a call and a response. I could not explain my purpose other than to say:

"I am writing a book of poetry." A minor purchase of property.

Poplar Island, n.d.
Courtesy New Westminster Public Library [acc. no. 2]

pages damaged restored discoloured stained or detached wholly or partially obscured by errata slips and tissue, etc., are refilmed for the best possible quality of the image. the following diagrams illustrate the method

Poplar Island pop patri individuated alike

lazaretto
Kamau Taurua, North Brother,
Angel our current

worse conditions of confinement

subjects of capture
property in the strictest sense

bound in a given moment
called to ground

unitary in the midst scattered

breathing
this next while a kind of evolution

stratifying dialects
from a strict sense of words

formal markers for ship makers

soluble paper ever sad
phonetic social generations and forth

demonstration parcels bought and sold repeatedly
as the record shows stolen

light comes up over the southeast bridges

normative, quieted

that a place told you it was   *bleeding into the snow*

cold seeps to bone
born and cut with no language to remember

storage pits, caches, the hanging lots for crows

as land sounds lean into sleet
cottonwood trees

in the dark of winter growing tips "see" light
                causing seedlings to bend toward the source

whiles before people disposed in a hundred-dollar hospital
corporeal lessons lean toward shared logics and finer beats

  for the old lamps to show the whips still stuck
    after centuries in the old wounds

pages to an opposite shore

to earth beneath here

an "I" on pavement or other words over
centuries of rotting matter

so sanctuary monoglot accent
island passed back into non-standard

trees suffer catenary curves of ivy and gossamer
signal lines tremble

sway and song put to order; to archive under English cloak

listening horizons burst new density this time

an "I" wants to pull a part as well
    words light rain

romancing words   *composed upon a bridge*
                       in the smokeless air

from the sky bridge
in the *golden* dawn pouring over wakening condos

    o'r supplanted industry

routes you give in strings and I take as ligaments

called to the surface revolution a minimal surface

the most minimal surface other than the plane

a bloom
a smile curved up into sepals awn-like petals

past the parapet widening to the throat
lingual bone thumbed to spine

riparian causeway to ocean

audible integrity bending moments cable-stayed

dark-eyed juncos
sited earlier at the annual camp

in turn this morning awake to
snow again after a better night's sleep
warmer and having prepared ample supplies

grease ready to move
us still here sitting awhile

bough-lined yesterday's divot I was born by the river
just like that river … running ever since. It's been a long time

draw in the learn by heart
years now, of seasons

presence passed by often
most often I see this at dusk

less in the hitch and turmoil of mornings
from that rare seat by the window

island or each spot on land
infinite and tractable

passing by
stones remember grandmothers

every point of loss
others here, we have heard of each other

handles
under poplars lore

colonial courts determined
peoples sway cease soar

the maps are not the territory, not these hills …

Grosse Isle onto the fever sheds
or as *Skwtsa7s* future remains
after gales tear the soil

the defence is national
natural

kept and sent subjects
armed to a place
static

invariants

there
and here
as long as the tongues thrive
tips swirl in a huff of cheeks

centripetal release

ecology down and up river
the *hə́ńqəmińəm* curls carried on

place is a while we walk on the bones of all time

Bill Vander Zalm revamped Woodlands Hospital Cemetery
the desecration of graves gave way to park activity
thousands distal dismember to old records traces now

The Queen's Park Hospital Society
holds the surveyed grid showing locations
where individuals are buried without upkeep to save money

there is a place (built over) at the southern end of Agnes Street

burial grounds (built over) of the present high school

being broken a constant

[we who do this all the time to we eroded are legible]

a stand in part for Woodlands previously:
the Provincial Hospital for the Insane, the Lunatic Asylum
and the cemetery associated with the former BC Penitentiary

windows too high / long road ditches / song for any us from here

To the following purposes only: Firstly, the sum of $75,000, or such less sum as may be found sufficient therefor, shall be given as a bonus to aid in the construction of a railway to connect the City of New Westminster with the main line of the Canadian Pacific Railway, to any such person or persons, corporation or corporations, as may be found willing and may be able to undertake the construction and maintenance of such railway upon such terms and conditions as the Council may, by resolutions, approve.

extinguishment of a right title is permanent
types of temporary use

to prove title
seasonal fishing hunting gathering

trails circle around
seasonal round

what is this test (*the maps are not the territory*)

peoples a regular use and occupation
tenures

every day the drive
economy of tenure holders

prospective enterprise
tenure holders

tree felled farm ship mine, permanent
jeopardy

peoples the declaration
traditional territory not reconciliation

provocative forestry provocative fishing

as the crown of ownership
values land

managers make decisions
to establish colony

officially spoken boundaries borders and property

along with his crew of men, descended
the river—named after him—

authority makes more paper

Saturn half a fist away saw
seared soared-up never thought about home

> *they do not have the mindset we*

log boom shores of land-title system
in harbour waters
communication
hereabouts

call the river the Fraser
call these now the river lots
plan to lease harbour nearby

transportation terse
surveyors cordoning river across to Brownsville

immediate transformation becomings start pinpoint

49°11'56"N, 122°56'3"w though the maps interpret

automatic breathe this next while a few centuries

morning glories in linnaeus's garden shine a corridor

sparks the red spindles annularly soaring flames of oily

brutality trunks' conditions, circle finer circles hole on

a plane spinal course run-through nerves recount of 1889

As settlement spread up the Fraser River an epidemic occurred in 1889. Because it was not connected to any other part of New Westminster, Poplar Island was chosen as a place to quarantine smallpox victims. In July, New Westminster Mayor John Hendry reported to council that "prompt steps had been taken to prevent the spread" and that a "good hospital had been created on Poplar Island to which patients as far as known had been removed" (City Minutes—July, 1889). $100 was spent to build the hospital. It is believed that many native people from around Vancouver were transported to Poplar Island during the epidemic and many may have been buried there (Wilkinson).

$3,396 spent to build The Royal Columbian Hospital

The Board of Management desire to accord a
vote of thanks to His Excellency the Governor
for a grant $2,500 00,
To the officers and men of the Royal
        Engineers, for the proceeds of a
        theatrical performance at their club,
        the sum of . . . . $354 50.
To the Chief Inspector of Police, for
        Granting the use of convict labor
        in clearing and grading town lots
        17 and 18, Block XXXI, the site
        of the hospital.
                    the growing import-
ance of the Colony, and the rapid increase of
our population, especially in the mining season,
        great necessity
General Hospital
An institution, when inaugurated, to be conduct-
ed on liberal principles, open to all deserving
patients …

great the future of the Colony may be, it will be
found that sufficient lands are held in trust to
meet all requirements, indeed we may reasonably
expect that the revenue derived from this source
hereafter will in a great measure defray the ex-
penses of the institution; but it devolves upon
the public to grasp boldly the subject and provide
a home for the indigent sick …

Now approach the subject in connection with
charitable institutions,
        always regarded as the most interest-
ing and necessary statement, viz., the financial
accounts.

from Koonspa at the tip of Lulu looking out on   Poplar
a plaque for the shipbuilding industry

no plaques on the starve of the old company

harm meets hand

yet, with these hard-times empaths, plaques are nothing
as the plagues were everything, if ninety percent

cared for continue

how industry to box stores luther core
the bridge sparkle shore to shore constant
burn of oil entering the Landing.   living for shopping needs

full desire

companies establish the mouth
to cost men to stop before
heading upriver

mine mercenaries vindicated
gold panning

warring sons of bankers
students of commerce

an important city / the former village

cultivated fields tracks trail sufficiency
of use

and occupation
demands
unarchived occupations

doing missionary settlers railway surveyors

I might say, we are very anxious to get this little piece
of ~~right of way~~ the reserve, as we propose
to erect our Gas Plant (Municipal)
and give the C.N. Rly. Co. a right-of-way through it.

a large group of men line the street
from the back door of the Land offices
they await an opportunity
to gain a piece of BC

tree island onto definitive tracks
blinks a haze of contact

shred through the built

developing
a bundle of wars

war rights of the Crown
power distributed

right to do things on and to

rights later to infringe already
the municipality

a witness to glory gone hot

all in all a grand day, a triumphant day
for the City bypassed by the mainline

invested heavily in its own railway
connections south tap the spikes driven

to a band of steel that completes the union

booming grounds near worker
cottages railway spur on
cannery facilities

access roads opposite
saw and shingle mills led to
evergreens thick at the stump

opening grassy meadows
fruit of roses sweet
for the thritic,
lupinus

bright greens of spring   *hum*
guttural quality wild sound

seeds random

lights methodically
turn on over the trails

urban lit sodium incandescent
't will be blue soon

history that no one
holds of interiors only imagined

homeless encampment slats
and garbage bags full of newspaper
dry leaves took the island one spring

another short while

an optical unconscious grasp at action

fore calm needs overcome
become intimacies become respiration

endowed by forces of nature, forces such as forest fire

darkened save the plumed out stack
bowed-out steam
system

evaporation microanatomy
adhesion, stumps

of cell walls end-to-end fibre forms
under the niddle of machine

streaming silver-blue roofs
trains below trains above

upper tacking texture lines
cracked floor of a dry river tracks

trace along side

nation majorities
idyllic sense of security

minorities   *pauseless*

respect
picking berries on the side of the road; an assertion of sovereignty

amenities under construction during winter
ice floes

ghostly the lines rise

for that ridgeline in the south
an echo of ridgelines north

sight shored
train in the snow at the docks

sweat to wools loading cargo
cannery crates of sturgeon and roe

packing it in at the company's dock
garden at homes
canning
moorage, a snag in the water
before plastic

   bridges, small-dot passages

centre-span arch under construction

devastated, may day, temporary stores
after the fire

ARBRE DE MAI COSMIQUE

pictured at the centre of the image: the *Onward*

Secondly, the surplus, shall be applied in the construction and maintenance of an efficient system of water-works, and of drainage and sewerage works in the City of New Westminster, and in the construction of a suitable City Hall, including the acquisition of a site therefor, if necessary, in such a manner as may be determined by any by-law or by-laws to be lawfully by the Corporation of the City.

New Westminster, B. C.
December 11th, 1912.

The Hon. Sir Richard McBride,
      Premier of B. C.
         Victoria, B. C.

Dear Sir:

   There is no use me telling you all over again my troubles.
I told you before.   Cannot you do something to help a poor
old Indian woman, the widow of Dutch Bill?   The City
people and the Indian Agent let Mr. Crane come on my
ground to make ways to build Boats, which I don't like.
   If I can get $2500.00 I will not stop here. Try and help me.
Please write me soon in care of Mr. Wm. Levine and oblige

             Your humble servant.

                                        her
                        Mary Agnes X Vianin.
                                       mark.

Public Works of Canada Plan: North Arm of Fraser River
Poplar Island to C.N. Rly Bridge

although there was a small population of

sawmills along the waterfront
on land side "smoke" stacks

beehive burners collecting ponds greenchain works yard
a machine is

many large stacks of cut lumber logs and squares
shipments to and from

unidentified workers of

Bucklin Lumber Company
Brunette Saw Mill
Capilano Timber Mill
Fraser Mills
Independent Shingle Mill Company
International Wood Products (Alaska Pine Company)
Mohawk Lumber Company
Pacific Coast Lumber Company
Pacific Veneer and Plywood (Canfor Mosquitoes fly out)
Rayonier (at one time purchased the island)
Royal City Planing Mills
Timberland Lumber Company
Westminster Paper Company (Scott Paper, Kruger)
Westminster Shook Mill

The Waterfront Esplanade Boardwalk

magnificent waterfront

band landless

etched public art on the river
across the river and the view from the river

arrived at Yi Fao

"great chiefs"

memories of colonial memories

royal affiliation rule of celebration
another May Day baby
queen

neighbours   *fresh water*   Sunbeam Gallery

"The Queen acknowledges Sir Edward Bulwer-Lytton's letter
… She has chosen 'New Westminster' for the name of the
Capital of British Columbia."

Imperial property. And whereas, the petitioners, in and by their said petition, further represented that they were desirous that the said map of the City ... in the Lands and Works Department, commonly known as the official map of the City of New Westminster, might be declared the public official map of the said City, with and subject to the amendments made under the Corporation surveys deposited, together with the field notes, by the petitioners on the twentieth day of April, 1880, in the Land Registry Office at Victoria, and praying that an Act might be passed for the purpose of carrying out the above objects.

a view down from the brow of the hill

sappers first

waterfront settle on

royal affiliations firm
industry poised necessity

curl dimensions   lest we

forget the colour of cranberry
marshes

cold, marrow-deep sound

felt
rumori dream am eristic

sand in the freshet of spring

stirs its names among other names, Stó:lō

fog rolls in and settles all afternoon whiles an autumn
moon that has lingered for days on the wane

over warships much more than ships
though ships themselves massive even and the building of

glaring holes from sky-sucking pipes the smoke and graphic
transact prod extraction some else enact heart thing cinder pairs

free berth autumn on a course out to sea past post, rudders thick

land-title system harbour hereabout shore
homes build centres

Irvings (keep on rollin' the nickels) act
new city bureaucrats

tenth avenue forms
attach through paper the booming eighties

three reserve parcels include thee island

hospital paternal
atonalistic department of wild cemetery

companies firmly departed affairs first and second

world war firms canning, vessels and munitions

southern portions and recording systems stacks

hey day may days post-fifty-five industrial

dense back when as globalized workers soldiers

at thirty dollars north arm draft densely

emblematic poplars rhizome ones a type march

homogeneous after cutting builds on industry pride

dead tree standing sunned and whipped dry
firewood lichen curls kindle

tree taken downtown
dragged carcass
across forest floor to blackened pit

dredge spoils

battle, an extreme form of dialogue
pain embraced by a loud river

ideality acts public out of order
wrested, returns

the mill turns around of its own free will

what makes the wind makes the rain

honour is epaulets learnt

hitch to hold
pronounce as uniform

problems depreciate
onward

Heaps Engineering
secure contracts manufacture
munitions the city's companies turned out
over 500,000 shells for the Imperial Munitions Board

to serve men
men serve

massage the gap

abstruse excesses

congenital insensitivity to pain

crude touch fibres carried
decussate at the level of the spinal cord

lexer flex parser bison the parser in human-readable
format context-free grammars

steady operations of simple rules the difference of epaulets

company that company war contracts
war efforts more shells for

men and women work day and night
like Vulcan Iron Works

for those may kill admirably, machine-gun
miles of fronts

eight million horses lost and dearest mules

afferent nerves

to an end entirely trenches a waiting sea
lines innumerable endless caught up in this starving wait

the we on top of prisons having never time spent

within thirty days the shipyard was open and running
all the trees from the island were cleared
a rough footbridge built across to the foot of fourteenth
from the working shipyard

IMB built:
War Comox, *War Edensaw*, *War Kitimat*, *War Ewen*

and a couple coal carriers after the war

"coal's percentage of the mining product value"

the view, looking down the launch ramp

launch of the *War Comox* from Poplar Island

War Comox after launch being guided by the *Samson*
onto *Samson V* sternwheeler nationally significant

museum snagboat and the world's largest tin soldier

at Dawes Ways wartime work began to take its toll

vote the Imperial Munitions Board to armistice

large wooden cargo steamers

WATER MAIN CROSSING

current fluffs of pollen cloud the air
at the PIPE LINE CROSSING
debris the spiders spin caught beneath the bridge

dominant was the machine shop that was once full

"Big Crowd Sees Columbus II Take the Water Gracefully
   at Dawes Ways"

heavy industry district under comprehensive development

off lorry road slick stagnant wood star shipyards rotten

sick greens in the ditch water complement dry, straw-coloured

embankments hollyhocks' invasive spatter coral-red as iron

anchor wood grain metal to touch it to touch the riverbed

as sturgeon feet from what millennium sand in the long basin

the seven-and-a-half-foot rise a million sandbags 1948 water

long gone sea post logistics trade letters never to return

plaques detail red velvet upholstering luxurious role of text

swam in the ocean for the first time at twenty-two
so buoyant

use of force model
most competitive class of assets, brokers in Victoria

a good picture of the scar, a good picture of the stars

luxurious role of textual radicalism

live with doubt and uncertainty and not knowing
live not knowing rather than having an answer that is wrong

steady operations of simple rules *the difference was epaulets*

The City sold the island for $20,000 to Rayonier Canada
Forestry

for years the trees grew back tall and thin
booms anchored around

processed trees   relations
by hands   await

struggle wanders
cohabitation   lichen lovers frosted and reddish
          wrested from you in struggle return to you in struggle

dead wood standing and fallen trees close in

the sound
having heard the sound of wolves

long and far gone

the colony

had grown a sense of permanence, a bluff of ever-present

It shall be lawful for the Corporation of the City ... to sell and convey all or any part of the said public squares or reserves, and public lands, granted as aforesaid and the Council of the said Corporation may pass by-laws, from time to time to determine what parts of the said property shall be sold, for what price, upon what terms, and may alter or repeal any such by-law; and any conveyance.

Hon. Sir. Richard McBride,
     VICTORIA, B. C.

Dear Sir Richard—

In reply to yours of the 20th. Inst., I would be very pleased to give Mrs. Vianan $2,500 to move off the Reserve, if it would be any use to do so, so far as the City is concerned.

You are aware that we have been negotiating with the Government at Ottawa for these Reserves for the last two and half years.   I also took it up with the Department when in Ottawa. When Dr. McKenna was out here he assured me that there would be no difficulty about it; but that the usual form would have to be gone through, and as they were negotiating with your Government in connection with Indian Reserves in the Province they thought it better to wait until some arrangement was arrived at before taking any definite action.   I think a word from you would settle this question without any difficulty, as Deputy Minister Pedley told me there were no complications in this matter, as the Reserves were being held for New Westminster and Brownsville Indians. There are no Westminster Indians, except Mrs. Vianan, and only a few at Brownsville.

I might say, we are very anxious to get this little piece of ~~right of way~~ the reserve, as we propose to erect our Gas Plant (Municipal) and give the C.N. Rly. Co. a right-of-way through it.

We are just about ready now to start work, and we have, as I stated, been urging Ottawa to act, and I think this would be a very good way of disposing with the whole question, by our giving Mrs. Vianan say, $2,500.

I suppose you are aware that all the buildings on the property belong to the City, and I might say Mrs. Vianan has a white man living with her; who, I fear, is looking for some of the rake-off that ought to go entirely to her, although, as you know, she is pretty well able to take care of herself.

I wonder if it would not be possible for you to just drop a line to Ottawa, suggesting that they settle all those Indian reserves, including Poplar Island, at once. We will pay a fair price, I should think $5,000 would be sufficient for the one or two families of Indians for whom these seem particularly to be held.   If you would, I believe that it would be settled at once; because Dr. McKenna himself is favourable to the settling up of the affair, and as we require them for Railroad and Harbor Development purposes there should be no difficulty.   I will be only too pleased to do all that I can on your request for Mrs. Vianan, and we have been watching to see that she has proper care taken of her;   but the man she has around there wont stand for anybody interfering with their affairs and she, apparently, has put herself under his protection. However, will be glad to hear from you on this point and have your views.

Allow me to thank you for your very kind wishes, and if I may, would like to wish for you and your family the very best of good things for the coming year.

Yours very truly,

John A. Lee

Thompson Nicola Regional District Library System

how the eye loves to rest on the water
determine to supplant the water
purchase a view of the water

taken from the ding
of the docks

looking east, looking west
looking northeast

an interior
view of the Golden Mile

early as a city

from the river, of new homes

to Poplar Island from the River Road

the view looking down the launch ramp

a pile of shingles mess of refuse once a roof
time pulls through each instant

as the leaves drop the light filters easier
reveals listening horizon

bursts of greenish-yellow
through branches blur

water surround, booming anchorage

softly viewed

hollow long perpetual job loss a bridge spectres

eyes with pain—laugh through ... conceal a squadron

bide a wee know a place you could throw a rock to
hinge your knuckles to hardwood roots

throw farther
a home shored up

listening to Abel Meeropol wit rumble
fret a concept hover frozen

in a spell of free berth the warmth loft
contingent on air the fabric composes, mixing it down

always proposing connections to the island
proposed developments

land rid debris
the island cut, eroded
it watches, were it watching

the shoreline burn another mill
rage a toss of flames cough of black smoke

built-upon shore again remnants
old firs and rugged deciduous

acidic soil salmoned trees are incredible
unbelievable

and don't we cut them down
sharply, smartly "mined or grown"

clean scraper-less skyline by the constant churn

rock-free berth yet to collect on space
packed in by this rushing

natural as the built post
post rots dock legs

in booms of tree carcasses
severed

weir rose and rings, I can count them
slaves chained to our tugboats

new path new construction
erosion flushes

floats of bright colours

slate sky oh fog that catches
in here valley lush at the core of static

stand up now, the wasteland to maintain
your houses they pull down
stand up now

your houses they pull down
to fright poor men in town

gentry must come down
and the poor shall wear the crown

since tyranny came in they count it now

to make a gaol a gin and to serve poor men therein

rather like Louisiana to Canada, somewhere

her father got a job in a paper mill until
he made enough to move back down

bought a home at 6 mile and Dequindre Road

fella on Cass Ave. kept on like a song

a while then the place called Flame Show Bar
on John R Street that last show Holiday did in Detroit
just weeks before. imagine. quality atolls far on

dwells in nepantla Belle beyond, hovering *with no feet*

oscillations feedback the dream keeps
a meal shared

on the porch out back, behind a safe kitchen
mid-afternoon play while the adults

metallic glitter

silence of Cage to the grizzled symphony-goer

spare sound texture sounds mm mmm
cultural sounds entrapment

never again silent even as extinction

acoustic wishes in alive
system

undocumented *hums* shares movement, floors

dark against the combined single
while puff out stacks

just steam fresh
still more the stream of silver blue

bear the initials I first knew
quick as nation
mimetic

record spirals hasten us to *bracing tasks*

Whereas, a petition has been presented by the Corporation of the City of New Westminster setting forth that the lands intended to be granted to the said Corporation by the "New Westminster City Lands Act, 1884," are therein erroneously described, and that doubts have arisen whether the said Act is effectual to vest the said lands in the said Corporation in the manner contemplated by the said Act;

speech acts wrested from
born by the river

matters talk and talk again
on the greyhound

again from time
Tk'emlúps te Secwépemc

bear in mind bodies people shipped
swelling

knuckles knot of solidarity
taken under wings and wings and wings

I have circled the same spot over and over

walls rise and fall to better walls

mortgaging future conditional
pledge of properties
outcome larger
drain
toward doubt

reverse time lapsed
residences un-construct
lots widen and fields un-furlough

seep marsh in, firs righted

cane recoils apparitional tangles
transparent

fluid congeals, opacity, a qualitative shift

timbre talk sharp

objects
quickly change

live
at the shoreline

velvet smells of summer

full sun
thermals birds circle

taciturn
lever hydraulics

reddish
cedar-rot orange

seem copper
circles run through it

free atoms split to render the egg yolk of autumn

reaches an art to alchemy artist fashion

the spine gilded paint syntax

brushed pigment
crafted golden light chromium dusk glides in

lovers of yellow fix a triumphant golden, not gold

no shine to the core impenetrable save tree-toppling ivy

rooted knots regulatory homage consistency
relative to the regulatory law infringed
limits

I dream I am there freely
a photo record looks like Herndl paints
                    who you are is where you are
said well

commercial deadening. awash, hangs, drips sweat
steady salt away patience for how this sound will evolve

at once, do this intersection
hold this

refrain from the fuck and hoard
or sale and clunky big block glare
of nothing that matters

this on is still on about an island
a giant wading away from shore

for sisters worth crest
what is work, what is a living

unarchival ones all labour

in cycles immaterial
this material is meaning what is said cows
after a long dry spell spindly and sickly

to give more—not what you got but what you can give

never knowing where
the dust of our grandmothers

righted up with love on a run boiling pour into unrest river

out longer ones longer begins to feel oh ones, feel
full touch down attach associate sensitize

feel pain, feel the evidence, feel free

feel *historical problems* trending present

tense fingertips feel a show of armoury green

move our aim we saw we and others have seen

for the wind to suck, for the sun to rot, for the tree to drop

be done and undone spring-like off the shuck off jive
gone apophenia

giving form to stimulus, not just some figure in the clouds

strong every day and every time with whole history out loud

but there is a man around there

has a white man living with her;
who, I fear,
is looking for some of the rake-off

ought to go entirely to her,
although, as you know,
she is pretty well able to take care of herself.

— — —

An Abandoned Factory, Detroit

The gates are chained, the barbed-wire fencing stands,
An iron authority against the snow,
And this grey monument to common sense
Resists the weather. Fears of idle hands,
Of protest, men in league, and of the slow
Corrosion of their minds, still charge this fence.

                              Philip Levine

Therefore Her Majesty, by and with the advice and consent of the Legislative Assembly of the Province of British Columbia, enacts as follows:

1. Section 1 of the "NWCLA 84" is hereby amended by striking out the words "coloured red" in the 11th line of the said section and substituting therefor the words "so named or described," and by striking out the words "deposited in the Land Registry Office" in the last line of the said section and by adding to the said section as so amended the words:

melq'ilwiye of sewn drum will and others
in the field grown purpose

swifts stir a swallow convergent evolution
reflecting

similar lifestyles
based on catching insects in flight

means without feet never settle
voluntarily on the ground

will cling to vertical surfaces
spaces of impermanence

tectonic heaving

gentler

did anyone take you under their wings?
the wings and wings and wings and vertical

I nation: red-winged blackbirds alight bulrush ditches

on wires in the morning doves are vicious scrappers
grackles mess the garden
cardinals in fields of soft wheat, corn, soy, hay repeat

this red, this pale yellow, this black

right laugh right laugh ...

I's a sensation we call colour
colour calculus strange simple
for a hundred shades each familiar hue fractures
late afternoon autumn contrary and builds to death

through migratory seasons we left lights on in windows
there birds lead the cause of ornithology

bracken nodes / cane-grazed riparian trees / *mitigomizhig*

roadside alongside history's other

dispossessed disposed to struggle
intellectual hills

up
over

facade possessed of glorious purpose: property

atom after oil
crisis after green after irradiated

displacement: talking about what is not present in space
and time

recursive language about language
productivity: use of language to create language

capacity
for displacement recursively, and productivity in language

The said lands and premises with their and every of their appurtenances shall from and after the passing of this Act be held and enjoyed by the said Corporation for a perfect, absolute, and indefeasible estate of inheritance in fee simple there in and every part and parcel thereof without any manner of trust, reservation, limitation, easement, proviso or condition, or any other matter or thing to alter, charge, change, encumber, defeat, or affect the same or any part or parcel thereof, and no person or persons shall as against the said Corporation or their assigns, have any right, title, or interest in, to, over or in respect of the said lands, or any part thereof, or to any easement in, order, or in respect, of the said lands, or any part or parcel thereof, whether by prescription, usage, or custom, or otherwise howsoever.

anticipatory force archivally replays
a point of view as slippery as itself
in an economy of fur-bearing animals

snow
how long

their scurvy
ignores spruce teas
acts of alterity   engulf

this is what you see at night
this road is a creek when it rains

ruined body
caroms into the margin

body comes to be again

bridge gathers passage
road obstruction forms ditches

feeding on garbage hundreds of distinct calls
two tones, crow call and crow family

study use tools
crowd open spaces in the tresses *years of sun*

glint in pavement

the mindset: we have just begun our fight

where violence routinely occurs generic
as patriarchal velocities
complex forms

the Postcommodity witness amplifies

inflammation

tested remedies distant and related
bruise the leaves to poultice

this view from above
like the crow was making, up in the distance

given to *tropistic*
survivance

toward light
collecting light

pressure
a quip of skin
catches in the briars
bloody then freer

not your typical foment

the use of language past
winded bleached individuation

toward conscious listened horizon

brand new logistics facilities for port-related business thousands
of square feet efficient layout
property features premium quality
insulated tilt-up concrete construction and systems

we are just about ready to start work. we will pay a fair price

great the future of the Colony may be

it will be found that
sufficient lands are held in trust to meet all requirements

indeed we may reasonably expect that the revenue
derived from this source hereafter will
in a great measure
defray the expenses of the institution but it devolves
upon the public to grasp boldly the subject and provide

Witnesseth, that in consideration of the sum of dollars of lawful money of Canada, heretofore paid by the purchaser to the Corporation, the receipt whereof is hereby acknowledged, the Corporation hereby grants and assigns unto the purchaser all that the parcel of land situate in the said City, being composed of Lot numbers in Blocks being part of shown on the official map of the said City according to a plan and subdivision—duly registered, together with the appurtenances thereunto belonging or in any wise appertaining, and all the right, title, interest, claim, and demand of the Corporation in, to, and upon the said premises; To have and to hold the said premises unto and to the use of the purchaser, his heirs, and assigns forever.

cut. securely ore
steel away Rosie
ain't I

closest on the train
the light bulbs, drops
my window

one-track construction delay
thorns bloody gums

the greyhound quality of love
kept in the loop
each crooked strange fruit
every stoop (we had)
we were used to
          domination and death
purpose

kept cages matched blue jack streets
corner mind the bloc fiscal ditches manner

wit thunder long after lightning the

prescriptive voice rather makes me cringe. But … yes.

ain't coca-cola it's rice—railways ... a summation

paid shill for Big Oil
fuel-injected big-block on cowboy boots suns
the Diamond Club where real men come to play

the basic industries

resort siphons

there in a cenote, few miles off the free highway
dissolution fracture flows catfish coffer

no asylum here winter is hitting
tent frame shed shack trailer SROs

service infrastructure extension cord coil
generations come to work in the cold lapis glitter

spanned a river in one stride

designated pathways prison guards shine
a light through bars check
alive and in your cell

multi-level means maximum valuation
cash-flow risk requirement return on equity

pathogens than is a plantation that is a si-
ting target

emerge all along languages' tip
mouth ulcers preceding settlement

laminated root rot refractive indices

hunger in neighbouring parts of the body
dull internal organs engage an outside

movement extends
sense location looking at or going to attend
place eroded by tugboats in the river's north arm

straight ahead in the dark shore verses away night
raft twenty-seven and a half acres

traditional variola vera droplets express

quarantine, and bury there the government
not taking the island's graves into account

warships were built view down the launch ramp

hundreds of workers walked the parcel
a rancherie, *raw roll up raw* connected corridor

over the north side's shadow moonlight streams
through a dark duppy comb of reeds, nerve-

ribbons flail angles strain out of water breathtaking

come out of time for this turn
silent shore just a burb to poplars

wild cherry cottonwood English ivy
black willow empathy

      great choiring branches far beyond

perches on the downed limbs

not a hand while it was writing
wilds the island not the factory
while there shifts they were family

figures with sloped shoulders sell newspapers
and bags of cherries on Jefferson Avenue

come out to Heidelberg Street for this sculpture
of stacked oil drums
"USA" stencilled on the side
partial sighs deep into patinas public purpose

open area strive starve up-and-come

zones to light across warm faces glassed-in places
all the vacant land the wide-open spaces we produced

every autonomy opposed and committed

birds kept off the crop

once harvest was done
harvest done worried some
worried men sing a worried song

songs common in the red humming
their whole lives prayers or persons likely to
become property spreading blacktop

master degrades the name
an owner tracked down and returned to the fields

"finance" is a slave's word   ima read

walk into any establishment
write your own newspaper

often hours rain curious converted speeches

on freedom's long road higher ground

rising wind dust began to rise again that wound
sucked ground rains a wind-funnelled lake

not enough and day after day

winter boots leak plastic bags incisor
cavities tire and sipe aggressive

bleeding-cause consciousness
the right to quiet enjoyment

the back a chitinous shield

sift the roving fragments attentively
subatomic cosmic clearing agents
incised spirals circle winch shapes
sinuous bands interlocking lace
so delicate it is weightless
hints of a watery primordial world
radiating appendages slender
cities like galaxies tend to cluster
spiral to elliptical oscura poured fire
rational primes disposed to struggle

river road for the duration securely ore
red slip surface and the orange clay below

not a question of knowledge but alertness

personified by the sovereign just as the sovereign is
personified by an oath faithful to her heirs' successors
faithfully observing laws and fulfilling citizen loyalty
not to a document such as a constitution, to a banner
such as a flag, or to a geopolitical entity such as a country

mercurially

split breeds tent city signal

alongside nuisance grounds and the garbage dump

dignity with fists embrace aging road allowance
people overcome to organize sensing purpose to life

banding poor and plagued to gain Inquiries
under bridges between ramps across from the parking lot

paved over remains of *spark from the old flints*

"Time is different at *Cankpe Opi*."

landscape and bread hooks' partial man digital detritus
offerings sky the stars

news broke her grace—great dancer reeds weave in water

rise on the stigmatic nature of bondage

benevolent abolitionists, remember your status
early frontiers and all matters of transport

unemployed workers attack the threshers

    moments of embodied risk

the flag or which banner

rite river pit lined with cedar boughs
wait daylight hours and leave only to eat

    sleep conflicting rebellions

by hand

curriculum who is classroom needs production
transitive havens

fresh lake walk wakes shoreline peppermint

tools under everything

anti-emblem entire freedom and any other light

prices will please the highest bidder. the purchaser shall be
entitled

and time shall be of the essence of the contract

when the cable snaps

found a few days ago
this side of the Serpentine
in an exhausted and helpless condition
he had dropped a bundle of blankets and a body of acumen

the proceeds of the sale of said lands shall be applied
feet of frontage

the slash burned as a precautionary measure, under control
at all times

spark from the old sound embers
at the shoreline of resuscitation. breath on tinder

hungry heavy equipment folds context
back into experience (then back out)

teeth make contact with the glass in the atrium
cracked and cut lips closest to you wood press back

isa sunk soil cut red clay south
                        in a merger step line

the black square becomes interesting only in context

pointillism in   *the anarchistic notion of*

                a society freed from work

fabled books for so   *imaginative militancy*
slices—rows and rows
shoot-you-then-remove-the-bullets   silence

to all you out there on the land   *good morning*

massa day done dreams run high got the
long count counts marked wall beside blade beside take

Shipyards on Poplar Island, 1917–1918
Courtesy New Westminster Museum and Archives [IHP 1317]

Acknowledgements

Some of these poems first appeared in: *Armed Cell* 2 (2012), ed. Brian Ang; the *Goose Journal for the Association for Literature, Environment, and Culture in Canada* (2014), ed. Sonnet L'Abbé; *Line* 76 (2013), ed. Amy De'Ath, Jeff Derksen, and Natalie Knight; the Oscar of Between salon series (2013), with Betsy Warland; *Poems by Sunday* (2014), ed. Daniel Owens; *Light-sensitive Matter* (2013), with David Garneau; *West Coast Line* 74, "Reconcile This!" (2012), ed. Jonathan Dewar and Ayumi Goto; and *Windstorms, Fathoms* (2012), with Ivan Drury.

Thank you to Ashok Mathur for facilitating residencies with the Centre for Innovation in Culture and the Arts in Canada for the Freemont Block "living art" centenary event (2011) as well as the REwork(s) in Progress (2012) and Reconsidering Reconciliation (2013), gatherings on the traditional territories of the Anishinaabe and the Secwépemc people.

"Poplar Island" is Qayqayt land.

From the Poplars is influenced by a number of texts and many more conversations. The conversations were not documented and I have not quoted from them. I am grateful for people's time and generosity, invaluable to this process and to my learning. The views presented herein are my own.

Sources

City of New Westminster Legislature. "1880, Chapter 19: An Act Respecting the Official Map of New Westminster." New Westminster Public Library: Heritage and Local History. Web. Accessed March 26, 2014.

————. "1884, Chapter 26: An Act to Authorize the City of New Westminster to Sell Certain Lands." New Westminster Public Library: Heritage and Local History. Web. Accessed March 26, 2014.

————. "1885, Chapter 29: An Act to Amend the 'New Westminster City Lands Act, 1884.'" New Westminster Public Library: Heritage and Local History. Web. Accessed March 26, 2014.

Glavin, Terry. "How Poplar Island Fell Off the Map." *Georgia Straight* (March 2, 2006). Web. Accessed March 26, 2014.

Hak, Gordon. *Capital and Labour in the British Columbia Forest Industry, 1934–74.* Vancouver: UBC Press, 2007. Print.

Lee, John A., to Richard McBride, December 28, 1912. Premier McBride inward official correspondence 1912. BC Archives GR-441, Box 48, folder 2. Letter.

Levine, Philip. "An Abandoned Factory, Detroit." *On the Edge.* New York: Random House, 1963. Republished in *On the Edge and Over: Poems, Old, Lost, and New.* Oakland: Cloud Marauder Press, 1976. Print.

Nienaber, Janice. "The History of Smallpox Quarantine on Poplar Island, British Columbia." vancouvertraces.weebly.com. Web. Accessed March 26, 2014.

Owen, Patricia, and Jim Wolf. *Yi Fao: Speaking through Memory: A History of New Westminster's Chinese Community 1858–1980.* Victoria: Heritage House, 2008. Print.

Royal Columbian Hospital. "Royal Columbian Hospital, Report of Directors, 1863." New Westminster. 1863. Microform.

Vianin, Mary Agnes, to Richard McBride, December 11, 1912. Premier McBride inward official correspondence 1912. BC Archives GR-441, Box 48, folder 2. Letter.

Wilkinson, Ken. "Poplar Island: A History as Thick and Colorful as the Trees." Tenth to the Fraser (October 24, 2010). Web. Accessed March 26, 2014.

Wolf, Jim. *Royal City: A Photographic History of New Westminster, 1858–1960.* Victoria: Heritage House, 2005. Print.

Woodland, Alan. *New Westminster: The Early Years 1858–1898.* New Westminster: Nunaga, 1973. Print.

Thank you

To my families near and far.

Jef Clarke especially, for first noticing the island and your work alongside. Shore
after the long hauls.

Love (and eternal rock) to the Prince George crew:
Aidyl, Paul, Pia, and Jules Jago, home to a first draft.

Mercedes Eng, for sharing the block. "allow it."
Ivan Drury, for your mistrust of words, legwork,
and necessary edits.
Garry Thomas Morse for listening to this project.
Steve Collis, once again, for seeing it through.

Ayumi Goto, Ashok Mathur, Betsy Warland, Carol Martin,
Cynthia Dewi Oka, David Garneau, Donato Mancini,
Greg Gibson, Hannah Calder, Hari Alluri, Harsha Walia,
Jeff Derksen, Jordan Scott, Juliane Okot Bitek, Junie Désil,
Larissa Lai, Marie Annharte, Natalie Knight, Neil Brooks,
Phinder Dulai, Proma Tagore, Renée Sarojini Saklikar,
Reg Johanson, Rita Wong, Roy Miki, press release diaspora,
and all my locals, on these unceded territories.

About the Author

Cecily Nicholson is the administrator of Gallery Gachet and has worked in the Downtown Eastside neighbourhood of Vancouver since 2000. Her work, both creative and social, engages conditions of displacement, class, and gender violence. She is the author of *Triage* (Vancouver: Talonbooks, 2011) and is a contributor to *Anamnesia: Unforgetting* (Vancouver: VIVO Media Arts, 2012).